Liberated Parents
Liberated Children

YOUR GUIDE TO A HAPPIER FAMILY

Other Avon Books by
Adele Faber and Elaine Mazlish

BETWEEN BROTHERS & SISTERS

HOW TO TALK SO KIDS WILL LISTEN
& LISTEN SO KIDS WILL TALK

SIBLINGS WITHOUT RIVALRY